Skyline

ONLINE SECURITY

protecting your personal information

UUID: f79f65c4-4d20-11e8-861f-17532927e555

This ebook was created with StreetLib Write
http://write.streetlib.com

Table of contents

INTRODUCTION 1

CHAPTER ONE 4

INTERNET SECURITY 5
DO WE NEED INTERNET SECURITY? 10
DEALING WITH INTERNET SECURITY 14
INTERNET SECURITY SOFTWARE
INTERNET SECURITY SOFTWARE 18
PROGRAMS 23

CHAPTER TWO 28

PERSONAL INFORMATION ONLINE 29
PERSONAL INFORMATION ONLINE –
SHOULD YOU BE WORRIED? 32

CHAPTER THREE 35

SOCIAL MEDIA SECURITY 36
SECURITY RISK IN THE SOCIAL MEDIA
ERA 43
SOCIAL MEDIA AND IDENTITY THEFT ... 47
THE DO'S AND DONT'S OF SOCIAL
MEDIA SECURITY 52

INTRODUCTION

One of your most precious possessions is your identity. Once you lose your identity to miscreants, it is very difficult to get it back. The world of internet has opened up an undesirable avenue through which hackers and cybercriminals access personal information for misuse. Protecting personal info, therefore, has become very essential today. There are many methods you have to use in order to ensure maximum protection of sensitive financial and personal information.

Always remember to be very stingy in giving out any personal info. Never volunteer any information no matter how much you are pressurized either offline or online. If you have to give information, find out how the information is going to be used. Unsolicited email messages must not be opened as phishing scams are one of the most commonly used methods to steal information. These emails can be

*blocked with the help of email filters.
There are many unreliable sites on the
internet waiting to flood your computer
with viruses in order to steal personal
information. Protecting personal
information is possible if you are careful
about the sites you open and surf.
Take all efforts to ensure security for
your internet connection and computer.
Protect your system with the help of
firewalls, anti-spyware and anti-virus
software.
Use your credit card for online purcha-
ses only on highly reliable and well-
known websites.
Always ensure you go through the
privacy policies on the websites you are
surfing. You will find details on what
they do with the personal information
you provide on the site and on whether
they install cookies on your browser to
enhance your browsing experience. If
you are not confident about the site, you
can opt to block the cookies.
Taking these precautions ensure you an
enjoyable internet experience. This is
also important for protecting personal
information.*

CHAPTER ONE

INTERNET SECURITY

To survive in today's highly competitive business environment, which is rapidly transmuting into a cyber village, businesses have to participate in the virtual world by using the Internet for not only emailing and chatting but also to tap the vast e-commerce market. However, on one hand, the Internet offers limitless opportunities for the entrepreneurs. On the other hand, Internet security and risk management pose monumental challenges for the corporate world today. However, countermeasures can be and must be taken in order to address the issue.

Before plunging into the sea of security issues that surround the use of the Internet, let us first look into the commonly followed definition of the umbrella term Internet Security.

Defining Internet Security

Internet security as defined "is the practice of protecting and preserving private resources and information on the Internet" (Internet Security). Hence, Internet security is fundamental to prevent a breach of e-commerce clients' trust and the resultant violation of privacy policies in order to avoid deformation of the companies' hard-earned corporate image. This leads us to the next section of our research assignment that discusses the scope of the issue under discussion.

Why Discuss Internet Security? The scope of the Problem

Information is exchanged via Internet use in the corporate world where people can communicate with each other and sell and buy products online using credit cards. Even confidential company data and many other secrets are shared via the Internet. However, this paves way for security issues, which make the "circuitous route" of the information being exchanged prone to deception, unauthenticated interruption, and other security risks. On the same account, Internet security has transformed into a major concern for all Internet users (Definitions of Internet Security on the web). Therefore, Internet security issues and risk management tips need to be discussed and highlighted for the benefit of the readers and the users alike.

Security-related Risks Associated with Internet Use and Management Strategies

Internet doubtless ameliorates corporate communication, "information sharing, market effectiveness and productivity" (Paliouras). Nonetheless, Internet use has often resulted in "security breaches with known or unknown undesirable consequences ranging from a crippled or hacked corporate network to a ruined reputation and costly litigation".

6

Consequently, the content of the emails must be filtered to prevent the above mentioned organizational issues. (Paliouras).

Risk Management via Content Filtering

"Klez worm" including other viruses that can seriously damage the computer system, "junk mail", shopping online using the Internet and visiting obscene sites at the organizational cost augment security risks (Paliouras). These risks can be reduced by making sure that employees avoid using company Internet services for irrelevant tasks. However, emails are highly important for business communication and "content filtering" is the best solution to manage security risks. "Advanced text analysis is necessary to prevent users from sending sexually explicit text and racial epithets or sensitive information to unauthorized parties. Lexical analysis is one way to cut down the leak of confidential information as most of these files include special words or phrases" (Paliouras). Moreover, "keyword searching and inspection" as well as "advanced image analysis" are some of the really effective weapons to reduce security risks associated with Internet use.

This is where the significance of information systems comes into play. With the aid of constructing appropriate systems and using adequate content filtering software, companies can block unnecessary and potentially harmful and insecure attachments from entering and infecting the computers.

A three-step approach inclusive of conceiving, constructing and consolidating been recommended by information systems companies in order to efficiently with security risks associated with the use of the Internet (Internet security challenges). However, the extent to which Internet use is secured primarily depends upon the company's "security awareness" (Katos). When electronically operating firms believe in cherishing their clientele's trust and therefore make every attempt to secure their operations via security checks, secured systems, and well-planned security policies, security risks tremendously plummet and the firm's reputation improves. Also, with security awareness, firms tend to be better equipped with latest advancements in the field of information systems.

Conclusion

Hence from the above discussion, it is evident that Internet security and risk management pose monumental challenges for the corporate world today. However, countermeasures can be and must be taken in order to address the issue. Those computer organizations that take help and make the most out of Information Systems are the ones that benefit the most in the long run. This is because Information systems offer a vast variety of security software, with the aid of which, organizations can reduce the risk of Internet use. Managing Internet security-related risks is no long an out-of-this-word task if adequate knowledge and timely application of Information systems are made available. Therefore, to address Internet security issues, the basic knowledge of Information Systems Fundamentals is essential. Moreover, extensive research and progress is demanded in the field of information systems in order to create "new defense mechanisms"

DO WE NEED INTERNET SECURITY?

The use of personal interaction in everyday life is a thing of the past. People these days rely on or even worst are now dependable upon the use of computers via the internet. In general, computers are being used to perform errands in business, financial transactions and even in private agendas from personal communication to shopping for groceries, paying bills, etc.

The only way of securing the users from other malicious internet users such as "hackers" is by using a good "internet security" program that can prolong if not deter the access of these prowlers on your personal security files. Prolong in a way that the user would be aware timely enough for him to make a start against these hackers.

These internet security programs pose as barricades that would block the access of hackers by means of pre-programmed agendas. They would scrutinize the potential hacker/threat as it passes through the random tests of the so-called security programs eliminating all possibilities of access once confirmed as threats' to the owner.

Each security program has its own level of protection. Usually, it depends upon the purpose. Some security programs are intended to deter "Viruses". A Virus, in general, tends to adhere to pre-existing programs of its hosts. They typically infiltrate a certain program disrupting its regular function as it slowly injects itself like a disease. Once it has completely infected that particular program, it will utilize the latter to infect neighboring programs as well until the whole system crashes and becomes inoperable.

A "Worm" is also another form of a virus. The worm injects itself to its potential victim in such ways that the host will not be aware of its presence nor the danger it possesses. It frequently imitates the hosts' system making it an integral part of the latter destroying it from the inside without the host even noticing it until it is too late, thus, is famous as the "backdoor" virus.

Malware (malicious software) on the other hand are types of programs that rouse the awareness of most internet security programs because of their source or origin. Usually, they are tagged as from "unconfirmed" sources. More often than not, they do not usually possess a risk to its hosts. Since they are the types of programs commonly used on the internet, they are the potential carriers of other formidable viruses.

"Spywares" in contrast, does not carry or possess any signs of a threat to the hosts. It generally disguises' itself as "helpful" programs offering simplicity and easiness in the use of the computer like browsing the internet making it very much appealing to the end user. Commonly free of charge, it normally requires personal data from would be users and sometimes, asking financial data making it a security as well as a financial threat.

Experts believe that having a fail-safe internet security program is not enough. It usually lies within the user himself' to achieve the full potential of the security program he utilizes. Typically, an internet security program needs maintenance to work properly. It is up to the user to regularly maintain the latter by updating its database and applications. An unmaintained internet security program is as good as not using anything at all.

Most internet security programs are obtaina-ble free from the internet. The only catch is that since they are free... the protections they provide are somehow limited. Sometimes, it is just propaganda on how to sell their products. They (providers) will allow you to download said programs in a certain predetermined limit. For sure it will be effecti-ve on some and simple types of viruses but not those complicated ones'... and once those complicated viruses had entered your com-puter system, the freeware you previously in-stalled will be requiring you to have an "upgrade"... which will cost to a large extent more compared to regularly purchased pro-grams.

Some internet security product providers made us believe that a good internet security program in itself is safe and reliable. These are mere "software" or programs that we use. What is important is the user themselves. The program would not stand for itself. It is how you use it counts most. Even a cheaply acqui-red security program together with an uncommon password will be indomitable as long as it's well maintained.

Internet security nowadays is considered a necessity and not a commodity. Many internet security providers offer numerous set of choices that the buyer/user can choose from depending on their preferences. Decide wisely... pick a security program based on your internet lifestyle... Buy what you believe you need and not what the providers want you to believe you need.

DEALING WITH INTERNET SECURITY

The internet is awash with many different kinds of threats and for many people, no introduction is required when it comes to the computer and internet threats. Most people have heard about the internet thetas and perhaps out of ignorance do not take any precaution to protect their computers and investments when working on the internet. The web as known today is used to collect, store, distribute information, for commerce, for entertainment and many other different activities. There is also the existence of companies, organizations, and individuals making their investment on the internet both in capital and time. Hence the inherent need to employ measures to deal with the internet security threats that face both the businesses and individuals on a daily basis when on the internet.

Let us explore the kind of threats and measures to take when on the internet. The most important facets of security will be those based on the collection of data; personal data and other sensitive data. The business transactions which are common to many online businesses and errors associated with these processes. The businesses demand that a bigger investment is made when instituting security measures to guarantees security. Online businesses need to have protocols to govern the handling and security of sensitive data, infrastructure which includes the network computers and all hardware deemed necessary for data collection and handling. Other aspects of security are the interactions of clients and servers, especially where information access is to be restricted. The deployment of measures such as the encryption and socket layered security come in handy and will be discussed. Basically, the major aspects of security including malware and virus detection and the deployment of the firewall will be tackled.

There are security threats which have been here with us and the internet threats continue to evolve and present even greater challenges for businesses. Security concerns continue to grow and they demand greater attention from all parties involved. This last year has seen the identification of malware which has actually baffled the security world owing to the nature of severity and complexity the malware has exhibited. Malware like Stuxnet and other malware which has hit the Middle East have just opened a different chapter in internet security. These threats were very complex and their capabilities were phenomenal in the manner in which they could steal and damage data. The new chapter which they opened was that of cyber espionage and state-backed cyber attacks.

It should be noted that many security issues are developed as a reactionary measure and hence the source of concern. But besides that, security should be tackled in a manner that prevents cyber attacks and wards off any other security threat. An overview of server security brings out the fact that for security to be guaranteed, then servers should be separated. The web server should be different from any other server. The web server is always a gateway to the internet and as such greater security measures are employed to secure all data held on this server. It is particularly true for online businesses. Before moving away from servers, client security is another aspect to be handled with a lot of security. Client security ensures that information is safeguarded from unauthorized access. Protocols are put in place to dictate the type and amount of data to be accessed.

So whatever the type of attack or internet security threat, it is important that there are systems in place to take care of these threats. In order to begin development of a cybersecurity plan, Internet threats must be understood and how protecting your business from those threats will augur well presently and in the future. Security threats are spread through social engineering, password cracking, port scanners, denial of service attacks and many other forms of threats. The measures to mitigate these unfortunate incidences are through web development best practices which involve ethical hackers identifying loopholes and appropriately sealing them to avoid attacks. Effective and strong passwords, encryption and security measures among a full collection of practices used to guarantee protection whatever the online investment.

INTERNET SECURITY SOFTWARE

Internet security involves the protection of a computer's Internet account and files from any form of attack or intrusion of an unauthorized user. Unauthorized access to a computer may occur once the computer connects to a network and begins communicating with other computers or accessing a malware-infected website through the Internet. To avoid this, it is recommended to set up a password and install an Internet security software. The following are some major Internet threats that can badly jeopardize a computer:
Malware
Worms
Bots
Spyware
Trojans
Viruses
The Internet threats mentioned above can be overlapped and combined, which can cause serious damage to your computer's system and personal files. These threats are the reason why they are made to detect and eliminate viruses and other forms of malicious attacks that can easily enter your computer. Internet security programs can be purchased or downloaded for free via the Internet. However, one should be careful in selecting the Internet security software that they will

use since some programs are not as effective as the others when it comes to detecting and removing viruses or malware. One should also be cautious when downloading such Internet security software since there are some existing websites that contain web links that would instruct you to install a security program for your computer when in reality it would actually install malware or even viruses on your computer. Most Internet security software has an antivirus, firewall, antispyware, as well as parental controls already integrated into one program to help you protect the following:

Personal information - Internet security programs contain antispyware, firewall, and anti-phishing protection to secure your sensitive data from creative hackers who are constantly using latest developments in technology to gain access to personal information.

Computer system - Internet security programs can shield your computer from being attacked by different kinds of viruses in forms of email attachments and other files, which may render your computer useless.

Family restriction - Parental controls are also included that allows you to filter and to restrict access to unacceptable sites or web contents that can also harm your computer. This feature can also keep your children from any possible online predators.

When looking for a reliable software, the follo-wing are some important criteria that a computer user must remember before downloading a particular program:

Ease of installation/setup
An Internet security software must be easy to install and to set up. It should have a clear and step by step instructions in order to avoid application errors or interfere with other programs on the computer.

Ease of Use
An Internet security software must be designed so that every user can be able to use the software regardless of their computer literacy. This also involves the program's interface as well as the terminologies used that will help the user to easily manage the software.

Other security features
A reliable Internet security software must have additional Internet security programs bundled such as email and IM scanning, anti-phishing, and parental controls.

Antispyware
An Internet security software must have an antispyware function that will protect your computer against adware, keyloggers, trojans, and many more.

Firewall

An Internet security software must have a firewall protection that will shield your computer from outside attackers or malicious Internet traffic. There are two types of firewalls namely:

Hardware - These are typically called network firewalls, which refers to external devices that are usually placed between your computer or network and your cable or DSL modem. Some Internet Service Providers (ISP) or vendors offer networking devices, such as a router, that already has a firewall installed. Hardware-based firewalls have the advantage of being separate devices, which are running on their own operating systems so they provide an additional line of defense against Internet attacks.

Software - These are firewalls that are built-in within the computer's operating system. If your computer's operating system has a firewall feature included, you may consider enabling it to provide an additional layer of protection even if you already have an external firewall. Antivirus
A security software must have the ability to continuously scan your computer for any harmful viruses. It is also important that the antivirus you are using are regularly updated to detect new viruses since these threats are constantly evolving.

Help and Support
Manufacturers should be able to provide support to its customers through FAQs, user

manual, or tutorials on how to properly use and maintain the Internet security software. It is also important that customers will obtain support through phone, chat, or email at all times.

INTERNET SECURITY SOFTWARE PROGRAMS

The 10 best internet security software programs have the best features and tools. And they effectively detect and block online threats like viruses, spyware, adware, rootkits, identity thieves, and hackers. And they also provide protection in areas that other security programs don't; such as social networking sites and online gaming environments.
But this is not enough to place an internet security program on the best list. And that's because many other programs that aren't on this list also provide excellent features and tools. And Panda Internet Security is one example; and has been certified by all the leading test labs and has some powerful tools that you won't find in other programs. However, what differentiates the best internet security programs is their combined security products which include antivirus, firewall, and anti-spam protection. Which together provide the highest level of protection from malicious software and hacker threats. And this is revealed in tests run by test labs like Virus Bulletin and West Coast Labs.
So here is our guide to the 10 best internet security software suites:

1. BitDefender

Tests carried out by AV-Test show that

BitDefender is the best at protecting against malware threats. Its antivirus software element is superior and has the Active Virus Control feature that monitors every process that runs on your computer. It has a two-way firewall which blocks threats from attacking your PC and also ensures you don't send threats to anyone else.

2. Kaspersky

Kaspersky internet security is packed with many features and comes complete with anti-virus software, parental controls and much more. It includes a virtual keyboard that lets you input your sensitive information without worrying about keyloggers. So it helps protect your bank details, usernames and passwords and shields your identity online. But Kaspersky is missing the Linkscanner feature for protection when using search engines.

3. Webroot

Webroot, like Kaspersky, provides cheap protection for up to three computers and in-cludes online backup. Webroot has the best antispyware program, Spy Sweeper. This software is rated the best by expert test labs. But Webroot has a disappointing firewall which has a complicated setup process and is time-consuming.

4. Norton

Norton internet security is a good program and uses innovative insight technologies to provide effective protection. Its all-around protection against malware threats is one of the best in the industry and it has passed all ICSA, VB100% and West Coast Labs 1 and 2 levels.

5. Eset

Eset has recently emerged as one of the best internet security programs. And it has the best tools and features for gamers. It provides excellent protection for external media and blocks pop-ups from gaming and video application. But its Help documentation lacks detail except when it comes to the most basic of setups.

6. AVG

We've always liked AVG for its effectiveness. And it has one of the best free antivirus programs that are also part of the internet security software suite. It also includes the Linkscanner feature for web safety protection and has one of the best identity theft protection options. But AVG is also lacking some important features that you find in other programs like parental controls.

7. Trend Micro

Trend Micro has many features and tools and some of them include backup, registry

cleaning, browsing history and cookie tracking. This is a broad feature base and is boosted by its antivirus, antispyware and firewall protection. Overall, Trend Micro is a good security solution but still lags behind many others.

8. eScan

eScan internet security is a lesser-known security product. But it's the effectiveness and features it includes that place it in the list of the 10 best internet security software programs. It has a unique user interface which is very useful and usable. And its detection rates are high, but its firewall is not one of the best.

9. BullGuard

BullGuard internet security has features like 5GB online storage space and a secure gaming mode which provide extra protection for your PC. The software is very easy to use and provides ample technical support. But it is missing parental controls which are now a common feature in other top internet security programs

10. ZoneAlarm

ZoneAlarm is last on the list of top security programs. And it includes virus, spyware and email protection and specific features for identity theft protection. And it is best known for its firewall which blocks some of the most dangerous threats online. But ZoneAlarm has a basic walkthrough feature which forces users to seek help elsewhere.

Summary

As mentioned earlier, there are other top internet security programs. And we recommend you check these out to make sure you pick the right software. For example, if you have children and protecting them online is important to you, then you want to make sure you pick a program with parental controls. And these features shouldn't just be basic; they should provide the most effective protection.

CHAPTER TWO

PERSONAL INFORMATION ONLINE

Each time you use the Internet to shop, transact with your bank or do any activity that needs you to send personal information, you are actually inviting intrusion of those whom you may not be happy to have around. In other words, you're making yourself a target for hackers who will always somehow find a way to make use of that personal information to serve themselves. Even when you've made your transactions a long time ago, it doesn't mean that details you've shared your credit card or bank account are necessarily gone. There will be traces and this is the part that most have been taking for granted.

Sure, there is encryption but it's not even a guaranteed way to totally eradicate the risk of your information being hijacked. This means that there are only two ways to address the problem: do not share your personal information online and, should sharing be inevitable, do something to remove all traces of that information. Remember that encryption only works when your computer is actually free from vulnerabilities or weaknesses. If it's not, then you're very much at risk. Just to make sure that nobody out there is going to use what you're only rightfully yours, have your computer fixed and safe from those vulnerabilities which could be easily exploited to make you a very easy target of identity theft and who knows what other cyber crimes these online hooks can perpetrate.

If it's impossible for you not to make online transactions involving your personal details, then you have to protect yourself manually by making sure that you delete traces of these details using your browser's options. The problem again is that it would be such a tedious task to have to clean up the traces because, after all, they're not one single virtual location that they can be controlled. There isn't even a single option that allows you to do the said task automatically.

You can make use of the SSL or Secure Socket Layer technology which also works with encryption except that, again, your computer could be exploited for its vulnerabilities and this type of protection may not work. Perhaps for the time that you have made your transactions, then you can deal with the dangers but the one thing you can do to protect yourself significantly is by preventing a scenario whereby you will be exposed to these online threats.

Prevention can be ensuring that your computer is free from vulnerabilities so as not to invite hackers. You can also install IP hiding software on your system so each time you have to shop or bank through the Internet, you can reduce the damage that identity theft can do. When your IP address is hidden, that means they won't have a way of reaching you and as long as you stay hidden, you'll be free from their clout.

Your Internet security should be paramount

when it comes to your Internet experience
and there is every reason for you to protect it.

PERSONAL INFORMATION ONLINE – SHOULD YOU BE WORRIED?

No matter whether you have an online business or not, you will be well aware of the need to protect your security whenever you go online. This is particularly important when it comes to any personal data which could be used by other people in some way.

Internet security is always evolving and improving, but that doesn't relieve you of the need to do whatever you can to keep yourself safe. The first step in the right direction is never to assume that the website you are going on has taken every possible measure to protect your information. That will always ultimately be down to you, and if you ever visit a website where things just don't seem quite as secure as they should be, it's safer to run in the opposite direction before you give up any personal information.

Any website requiring you to log in for some reason should always have a secure login screen that you can use. If it doesn't then anyone with the right knowledge could hack into the website and intercept the information you are logging in with. Always look for the secure padlock symbol and the https:// before the website address that indicates you are using a secure connection.

But personal security can be compromised in

other ways as well. Take the proliferation of social networking sites for example. These always require you to choose a screen name (a username if you prefer) and a password in order to access your account. Never use your own name or a version of it if you can possibly help it, and try and choose a different password for each website you join as well. It might be difficult to remember them all but it keeps your personal information safer in the long run if you do.

The worst sin is to use the same password for every single online login - from your bank accounts to your MySpace account. This is simply asking for trouble. A so-called ethical hacker would have a field day hacking into your computer and showing you just how much damage that single 'easy to remember' password could do in a very short space of time.

It seems then that you should be worried about putting personal information online, but that isn't always the case. It helps enormously to keep your wits about you and make sure that you are inputting your information over a secure connection whenever necessary, as well as keeping your logins secure and away from prying eyes. It certainly helps to have a good memory in this respect, since you don't want to write a huge list of them down in case anyone should find it.

In the end, you are responsible for your personal information and for keeping it safe. Most online security breaches occur as a result of people not taking all the steps they should be taking to keep themselves safe -

and that is the hardest way to learn this particular lesson.

CHAPTER THREE

SOCIAL MEDIA SECURITY

As well as individuals, companies large and small can be the victims of lax social media security. Accounts have been hacked, changed and used to spread political and scatological messages. Brands have been besmirched, and customers and prospects lost.

While large international corporations and other major players may be able to recover from these kinds of attacks easily enough, for the small business they can (and have) proved fatal.

So how can you counter these threats? Getting out of social media is not a solution. More and more people are using this kind of media to follow companies and brands, to talk about them, and to decide whether to buy their products or services. The role of social media in marketing is expanding conti-nuously and is set to stay. In fact, it looks set to eventually overtake more traditional sales tools.

The reality of the threats is that most of the breaches of security that have happened so far were due to the business owner or an em-ployee falling for simple scams... by opening suspicious emails or clicking through to rogue websites without a moment's hesitation.

Here are a few simple things you can do to protect yourself and your business.

Education and training

You or your staff may lack the caution needed to use networks securely. The only solution in these circumstances is education and training.

Structured social media education programmes that deliver training on the use of special tools and how you can do so securely are available. These come in a variety of formats, from brief how-to manuals to webinars.

You can find programmes that fit for your business and financial resources through Google.

Malicious links are a common way in which accounts are compromised. Caution is best, especially if links lead to pages that ask for usernames and passwords.

Thus a fundamental part of these educational programmes is training in how to recognize suspicious messages, emails or links that could act as a gateway into your systems for a hacker.

In addition to improving basic security, these programmes can also help improve the overall performance of social media campaigns. Indeed, many of them deliver training in the more advanced aspects of social media such as attracting new clients.

Protecting Passwords

If you and a member of your staff are sharing social media activities, you are likely to be sharing accounts and passwords. The more accounts you have, the more the passwords

that will be shared.
How can you keep these passwords secure?
The answer is... with great difficulty. Here's
what you need to do:
First, you should create strong (complex) passwords, rather than relying on simple, very
common passwords such as 12345etc or
password. Password generating tools are
available.
Secondly, you must make sure that
passwords are never stored on shared
computers, on mobile phones or in emails,
nor on post-it notes or other scraps of paper.
Complex passwords can be hard to
remember, especially where several are in
use. You can reduce the number of
passwords your staff uses by ensuring that
they sign into your firm's accounts using the
same username and password as they use for
their company email account.
This has the additional advantage that, should
an employee leave, their access to all
company media can be disabled in an instant.
A disgruntled employee can wreak havoc on
your social media accounts if he or she still
has access.

Centralising control over social media

Most people and businesses, even the very
smallest firms, will have multiple accounts on
many different networks, eg, Linked In,
Twitter, Facebook, and so on.
Maintaining control over several accounts can
be difficult and time-consuming, especially if
your company includes several people who

are involved in creating tweets and posting updates.

The first thing you need to do is to undertake an audit of all your accounts, noting who manages them and who has access to them.

Then you can close-down any accounts you don't need and remove permissions for the remaining account from any employees who don't need them.

Once that is done, you can consolidate these accounts within a social media management system. An SMMS will allow you:

write messages and publish them to several accounts on several social networks from a single interface or dashboard

monitor all social activities from one place (thus simplifying a time-consuming task).

Several well-known SMMS are available. Most operate on a freemium basis, ie basic services are free to users but additional services are delivered on a paid basis.

A good SMMS will have built-in malware tools to notify users when a suspect link is clicked. A secure system will also notify you if suspicious activity is taking place on your accounts, giving you a chance to shut-down a possible security threat.

Paid social media, such as Facebook's Promoted Posts, has made the need to bring all social media under central control using an SMMS all the more urgent. Imagine a situation in which you invest tens of thousands of Euro or dollars into Promoted Tweets on Twitter and someone who hacked your account ruins the whole campaign with an offensive tweet. The malware tools built into an SMMS should be able to prevent scenarios like this happening. In addition, such an SMMS should also be able to monitor the outcomes of paid social media without requiring the additional passwords usually associated with paid media platforms.

Message approval

A mistweet or other mistake on social media can happen easily. The only way to avoid these kinds of errors, which can seriously damage your reputation, is to set up an approval process that must be followed before a social message can be posted.
Of course, a formal approval process is only applicable if more than one person is undertaking social media activities. In these circumstances, the process will probably be vital in order to ensure that the standards you expect in your social messages are achieved.
The simplest approval process is just to allow another person to review a tweet, message or update before it is posted. Good social media management systems should include an approval process for all social media messages.
As well as allowing the content of posts to be checked, an approval process means that typos and spelling errors can be corrected and links checked. The process also gives you and your employees a chance to learn from each other as suggestions and corrections are made.
An approval process will dramatically reduce

the likelihood of a major social media crisis. However, it will not guarantee that nothing goes wrong.

Disaster recovery

Mistakes happen. No matter how many security measures you undertake, there is always a chance that something will go wrong and an inappropriate message will be sent, either because something was missed by accident during the approval process or a hacker gained access.
So, what can you do if the worst happens? The only answer is the boy scouts' motto: be prepared.
'Being prepared' means that you and your employees must have a specific plan on how to respond quickly and effectively when a crisis erupts. As crises tend to be unpredictable, this plan must be flexible.
You should test and evaluate your plan to ensure that it will actually work in an emergency. You also need to practice the plan so you and your people know instinctively what to do.
Social media happens in real-time so you need to respond in real-time. Social media, in fact, can help you respond appropriately. This is best done using a tried and tested social media management system.
A good SMMS will enable you to monitor how your customers, prospects and the public at large are reacting to the issue so that you can respond with appropriate messages.
Social media allows you to reach a massive

number of people quickly so you can tell them about the problem and how you are working to resolve it. This can increase your credibility with customers and prospects and the public at large... which is what social media for business is all about.

SECURITY RISK IN THE SOCIAL MEDIA ERA

Everyone is joining in the social media craze, even the public figures of our times. With hundreds of millions of users, from school going teenagers to presidents, to footballers and musicians, from small and medium companies to large corporations, many people use at least one of the various social media, like Facebook, Twitter, LinkedIn, MySpace, YouTube among others, to either connect with friends, network and make friends, for promotion and public relations and for marketing purposes, among other benefits.

Social Media has changed the way we interact and communicate; we can now stay in touch through Facebook with friends, fans, and clients. We can pass on information quickly in a way we have never done before through Twitter. Through social media, we can reunite with lost family members and friends.

For individual users of Social media, the biggest challenge is that People drop their guard and share personal information and secrets on Facebook, including details they would not easily shout out in the streets, share on national TV or Radio. Within their social networks, they feel safe surrounded by people they know, like and trust, like friends and family. This opens possibilities for identity theft and could be used as an avenue for Social

engineering - a practice of gathering information on someone for future criminal use.
There is also the threat of Cyberstalking, where a user can be electronically harassed or
abused, as well as issues of solicitation of
minors for sex, or gathering information on an
individual in order to harass them later with
that information.
For Enterprises and corporations that have
internet access and allow the use of social
media by employees on the corporate network; the risks could be even bigger. While
social networking has become pervasive
across organizations, there are very few security restrictions governing its usage. Not only
could uncontrolled use of social media lead
to misuse of internet resources, but could as
well lead to productivity loss, as employees
spend more time on social networks, instead
of carrying out official work. Social networks
could be used to introduce malware like computer viruses, on corporate networks. For
example in September 2010, "onMouseOver"
the Twitter-based worm pummeled users
with pop-ups, spam and pornographic tweets
and then re-tweeted them to everyone on
their contact list.
Social networks can also be a route for data
leakage, where they can be used to leak company trade secrets, and lead to
confidential/sensitive data loss or leakage.
What's more, there's a disconnect between
traditional information security practices and
the demands of an increasingly youthful
workforce that feels entitled to use personal
technology and social networking in the office.

So what can be done to curb the risks of social media usage and enjoy its benefits with fewer worries? To begin with, there is a need for social media users, to be vigilant and not share any information they could not easily share with the general public. On top of using a stronger password that can't easily be guessed, we should take advantage of the options available within the social media themselves to assist with reducing the risks. Major social networking sites now support identity management functionality. For example, a security application called mysafeFriend gives Facebook users a way to validate the identity of potential friends.

Parents need to guide their children on safe usage of the internet and appropriate behavior when online. Just like you would not let your children chat with any stranger in the streets, why should you allow them to freely connect with cyber strangers, who could be closer than you think? For Organizations, there is need to have an administrative and technical approach to the problem. Companies should come up with internet usage policies at the workplace that have a component dedicated to social media usage, for example specifying what time employees can access social network sites, so that employee productivity is not affected. There should be awareness training for staff as well on risks involved. Companies could make use of available technology to assist with web content filtering against malware like viruses and infected links shared through social networks. As social networks become popular, there is a need for individuals and corporations to be aware of the risks, and of the fact that Scammers and cyber-criminals today have their sights trained on users of social networks.

SOCIAL MEDIA AND IDENTITY THEFT

Social media is teeming with opportunities for identity thieves, and most people are unaware they're even at risk. Consider this: 54 percent of social media profiles have been targeted for identity theft, 15 percent of people have had their account accessed without their permission, and 70 percent have been asked to visit a scam website via private message. What are you doing to prevent identity theft on social media websites? A study shows that 93 percent of Facebook users share their full name on their social media profile, 60 percent share the full names of family members, and 33 percent share their employer information. Although you are prompted to provide your full name, the city in which you live, your date of birth, and other personal identifying information when you sign-up with a social networking site like Facebook, you don't have to supply it. However, publishing this information for all the world to see makes it easy for an identity thief to get to work.

How Social Media Increases Your Chances of Identity Theft

It's no secret that social networking plays an important part in many of our lives. We share status updates, stay in touch with old friends, share family photos, share links to interesting content, in addition to a wide variety of other uses. While this is a great way to stay connected and has made the world a lot smaller, social media profiles and the tidbits of information people share--such as saying when they're out of town--make them prime targets for identity thieves.

Online games are breeding grounds for social media identity theft as well. These games often offer incentives to players to fill out forms with their personal information. Some have even been known to ask users to fill out a loan application, which requires supplying their Social Security number. With users sharing games among friends, hundreds--if not thousands--of gamers can become victims before they've even signed off for the night.

Protecting Yourself From Social Media Identity Theft

Luckily, there are many things you can do (and not do) to prevent identity theft on social networking websites. Here are a few easy ways to protect yourself from identity theft while still using social networking to stay connected and have fun online:

• Omit personal information: Your personal information is not required to start a social media profile. In fact, you don't even need your real name. Instead of using your full name, use a nickname or other alias. You also don't want to provide additional information that helps identity thieves, including your date of birth, birthplace or hometown, address, and employer information.

• Use privacy settings: Most social media profiles allow you to select who can see your profile and how much they can see. Set all personal information to "private" and only allow friends to access the information.

• Don't be friends with everyone: A lot of users who accept friend requests from anyone who sends them one. For all you know, one of those new "friends" is an identity thief trying to steal your information. Instead, just like in "the real world" you only want to share private information with people you know.

• Don't tag locations: If you're out of town or away from home, don't tag yourself in a location. This tells identity thieves where you are and can increase the chances of your home being broken into while you're away. Unfortunately, identity thieves are waiting to pounce around every online corner. Providing even the most basic information makes you vulnerable to social media identity theft, which can result in huge financial losses that can take years from which to recover.

Get Identity Theft Protection

When it comes to social media identity theft, becoming a victim is a "when" not "if" situation. In addition to taking the precautions discussed above for your social media profile, the best way to prevent identity theft is to sign up with a protection service such as ID Theft Solutions so your identity will be monitored and even recovered when it's sto-

len. There are also many excellent free resources for getting specific tips you can start
using today to prevent this growing form and
dangerous type of theft.

THE DO'S AND DON'T'S OF SOCIAL MEDIA SECURITY

Before anything else we would start with the quote, "Safety is a cheap and effective insurance policy". In any angle, this quote is really a fact and applies to each one of us in our day to day battle with what we call life. It is indeed a cheap but effective way of being safe not just physically but also, mentally and socially. Sometimes, when a person is too much pleased they intend to forget a lot of things, including their own safety. Well, we can't stop these problems and threats but, we could avoid or prevent it to happen. Currently, with the great number of emerging Social Media sites like YouTube, Facebook, Twitter, LinkedIn and a lot more to discover, we are exposed to all possibilities. These Social media platforms bring along with them advantages where we could greatly benefit from it and also disadvantages. Advantages mean Social Media builds a good relationship with its users among other users too whether it's your long lost friend or mutual friends. It helps a user search for relevant products/services, introduces and promotes business to fellow users and look for some productive details or data and foundation for putting up a business, small or medium size.
Now, we focus on its disadvantages and flaws. Bear in mind that the main purpose of these Social media platforms is to be exposed

socially to thousands of people around the globe. Problems may occur if we allow them to happen, of course. In fact, there had been reports about identity theft that is very alarming and could possibly happen to anyone who's not aware of it. Now, how can we prevent these from happening and avoid being a victim? Here are some must Do's and Don'ts before, while and after we are using any Social Media platforms:

Do Promote-Promote your products or services to prospect consumers/clients. Post only relevant photos, captions, details and company's general information with great care.

Do not Give Away Too Much Info's-Only relevant information shall be given to your audiences. Do not give unnecessary details about yourself or your company.

Do edit your privacy settings-There are hundreds of different Social media platforms and each of them provides a Privacy Settings that could be the first and foremost step in securing your or your company's privacy. Change/edit it to what your business needs suit best.

Do not Forget To Check-As you logged in (especially when using a public computer) or better yet, always check the logging in details first. Uncheck unnecessary box/boxes that you don't really need. Ex. Uncheck the box that says, "Keep me logged in".

Do Keep Your Username/Passwords Secured-What are the purpose of making a username and passwords if you don`t keep it safe? Never give these details away to anybody.

Especially if you are requested to such action over email. Banks and Insurance companies will NEVER ask you to enter these details by email.

Do not Underestimate Discipline-Discipline is also a vital guide to each one of us. If possible, don't visit and logged in on suspected and unsecured sites. Actually, being well disciplined and control over unnecessary actions would surely guide you in avoiding mistakes that could lead to your or your company's downfall.

Do Invest in Securing Your Sites- There are different security and verification certificates. Trust seals from Company On Net, Verisign Trust Seal, Trust Guard etc. SSL certificates from Digi Design, Geotrust, Verisign and malware scanners like McAfee SiteAdvisor and Hacker Safe. Spending money on these tools is also satisfying and gives greater security.

www.ingramcontent.com/pod-product-compliance
Lightning Source LLC
Chambersburg PA
CBHW070900070326
40690CB00009B/1932